IMAGES
*of America*

# SEATTLE'S
# LUNA PARK

This photo postcard makes a prop of one of Luna Park's major rides, the Shoot-the-Chutes. "The chutes," as it was commonly called, made its debut at Coney Island and became the amusement industry's first successful water ride. It involved racing down a track in a gondola and into a lagoon below. Photo postcards such as this were popular souvenirs at the time. (Author's collection.)

ON THE COVER: This photograph was taken facing east, toward Elliott Bay, from the starting point of the Shoot-the-Chutes. From roughly 100 feet above Luna Park's midway, gondolas slid down the left track into the pool below. The boats were then hoisted back to the top along the track to the right. In the background stand the oscillating swing and the Great Figure-Eight Roller Coaster, the reflection of which can be seen in the chutes' lagoon. This image was captured by Seattle photographer Otto Theodore Frasch. (Author's collection.)

IMAGES
*of America*

# SEATTLE'S
# LUNA PARK

Aaron J. Naff

ARCADIA
PUBLISHING

Published by Arcadia Publishing
Charleston, South Carolina


Library of Congress Control Number: 2011925218

For all general information, please contact Arcadia Publishing:
Telephone 843-853-2070
Fax 843-853-0044
E-mail sales@arcadiapublishing.com
For customer service and orders:
Toll-Free 1-888-313-2665

Visit us on the Internet at www.arcadiapublishing.com

*For Joshua Edward Carlson, 1978–2008.*
*We'll always be Timberbeasts.*

# CONTENTS

Acknowledgments                                                          6

Introduction                                                            7

1.   Seattle's Coney Island                                             9

2.   The Nation's Greatest Playground on the Pacific Coast            33

3.   Pioneer of the Coney Island Style                                65

4.   The Wild Scotsman                                                75

5.   The Longest Bar on the Bay                                       87

6.   The Cost of Big Amusement                                        99

7.   Last of Luna Park                                               111

Selected Bibliography                                                126

Index                                                                127

# ACKNOWLEDGMENTS

There are many whose efforts and guidance made this project possible. Most of the photographs appear thanks to the diligence of Sarah Frederick of the Log House Museum; Carolyn Marr of the Museum of History and Industry; and Nicolette Bromberg of University of Washington Libraries, Special Collections.

Robert Abrahamsen, Derek Fetters, and Terry Johnson, even after applying much ink to early drafts, remained encouraging. Ray Simmons, Charles I.D. Looff's great-grandson, shared his family's history. Roland Hopkins, editor of *Carousel News & Trader*, took the time to hunt for photographs in spite of his own looming deadlines. James R. Smith shared the photograph collection he used for his book, *San Francisco's Playland at the Beach: The Early Years*. Ephemera collectors Michael Fairley, Dan Kerlee, and Michael Maslan made available many images for this project.

Thank you to all of my friends and family, especially my parents, Ken and Kathy, and my sister, Heather. Though perhaps baffled as to why I took such an interest in a defunct amusement park, you were wholly supportive. I could not have done this without you.

# INTRODUCTION

Near the close of the 19th century, the innovations of industry converged with the demand for public entertainment and ignited a golden age of American amusement parks. Along the East Coast, parks such as those at Coney Island captivated the public with mechanized diversions that gleamed with electric light. Employing machines for the purpose of pleasure rather than labor, these attractions invited patrons to share in an experience that has cemented the amusement park as part of America's cultural heritage.

Such a park opened along the shore of Elliott Bay at the north end of Alki. Billed as "The Nation's Greatest Playground on the Pacific Coast," Luna Park offered contraptions and oddities found nowhere else in Seattle. Its boardwalk was lined with the most popular amusements of the day, some of which towered over 100 feet in the air. The park reflected Seattle's ambitions to be a great American city, as well as the decadence that had earned it a somewhat unsavory reputation.

The year 1907 was transformative for Seattle. The Klondike gold rush had pulled the city out of economic depression, as Seattle had been the last stop for prospectors seeking their fortunes and the first stop on their return. Gold seekers and every type of business that could profit from them had poured into Seattle. Hardware salesmen outfitted prospectors with all they would need to strike gold, and saloons and showmen offered them ample occasion to part with their earnings. It had been a financial boon for the young city, but it was not until a decade later that Seattle truly began to blossom.

In 1907, Seattle annexed five outlying towns, nearly doubling its size. A number of Seattle landmarks were opened, including the Moore Theater and Pike Place Market, which is now a famous tourist attraction. Ground was broken for the Alaska-Yukon-Pacific Exposition, the 1909 world's fair held on what is now the University of Washington's campus. A great American city was taking shape.

The resort area of Alki, with its long stretch of beach, was a prime location for an amusement park, and the area's rapid population growth promised a considerable clientele. West Seattle, however, was a rigidly moral community. Amusement parks, in part because of the lurid tales of Coney Island, had been stigmatized and were considered havens of debauchery. There were concerns the proposed park would sully West Seattle with vice. The city council approved the project, though, thinking it would be a draw for the local real estate market.

In June 1907, Luna Park threw the switch on thousands of incandescent lights and opened its gate to an immense and eager crowd. The park's wonders indulged nearly every human impulse and represented the abundance and prosperity Seattle had long sought. The park hosted exhilarating rides and seemingly endless concessions. Daredevils dived into undersized tanks and clung to rope slides by their teeth. Swarms of people splashed along the beach. The band organ resounded late into summer nights. For a 10¢ admission fee, visitors were treated to constant spectacles, and all could be as carefree as children.

There were rumors, however, of a sordid side to the park. Once the project had been approved, the park's developers convinced West Seattle's city council to grant them a liquor license. Luna Park was to offer "the best-stocked bar on the bay." Citizens were livid and now had another incentive for annexation into Seattle, whose mayor had promised to stamp out vice. West Seattle filed annexation papers days after Luna Park's opening. The park was targeted by anti-saloon campaigns. Its bar and dance hall were associated with a mayoral recall and were frequently raided under the new administration.

In its inaugural season, Luna Park was a novelty. In its second season, it was the launch site of Seattle's first manned flight. Luna Park's third season coincided with the Alaska-Yukon-Pacific Exposition, giving the park a final surge in attendance. Visitors from across the globe walked its midway. Seattle earned worldwide attention hosting the fair, and after its conclusion, the city continued progressing while Luna Park began to fade. Its rides became quaint, and attendance waned. Finally, the gate was closed and the lights went dark.

Legend holds that anti-saloon interests shut it down, but Luna Park's closure had many causes. Newer attractions in the area contributed to its static attendance, as did the injuries that were becoming more common. One patron slipped headfirst down the Shoot-the-Chutes and snapped his neck. Another was injured with a faulty mallet he swung while playing a game of chance; he filed a lawsuit. The partnership between Luna Park's managing companies was strained as well, which also resulted in lawsuits. One owner eventually sold his interest in the enterprise. The park's next season was its last.

The natatorium and dance hall stayed open for almost two more decades and were the last remaining structures on the nearly vacant pier. The natatorium had been given the name Luna Pool, but it was still called Luna Park, even by those too young to remember the carousel. The natatorium and dance hall remained popular venues for recreation and social engagements. They were also the targets of federal liquor raids, one of which led to a pursuit by boat. The former pleasure pier became an area landmark, a relic from one of the city's most prosperous eras. Then, one April morning, it was devoured by flames.

Luna Park has long since vanished from the shore of Elliott Bay. Yet in spite of its brief existence (and perhaps partly because of it), the park has become a local legend. Its history is sustained by organizations, such as the Log House Museum and the Museum of History and Industry; local businesses, such as Luna Park Café; and the Luna Park neighborhood of West Seattle. They hark back to a time of bowler hats and wasp waists, a time when a hopeful city emerged as a flourishing metropolis, and when Luna Park was "The Nation's Greatest Playground on the Pacific Coast."

# One

# SEATTLE'S CONEY ISLAND

Since as far back as the 1890s, Alki in West Seattle has been compared to New York's Coney Island. When Seattle's first white settlers landed on Alki in 1851, they quickly found the west side of the bay too shallow to bear a port. But this shallow beach made an ideal summer destination, particularly near the turn of the 20th century when beach bathing caught on.

In the winter of 1906, at the northern end of Alki Beach, workmen began driving pilings into the tideflats. In a few months, a peculiar structure took form—an immense pier bearing an arrangement of stark white, cone-roofed buildings. At one edge stood a careening framework of timbers and a skeletal tower with radial arms just beyond. By that spring, the aim of the endeavor was apparent.

Luna Park was to be Seattle's own Coney Island–style amusement park, offering a jumble of concessions that had garnered notoriety for the East Coast resort. The new park was advertised as the largest boardwalk on the Pacific coast, home to a gigantic display of world-famous features. The midway was lined with exhilarating rides, games, sideshows, and theaters. There was indoor bathing in addition to acres of surrounding beach. Luna Park was an altogether new type of attraction for the city.

In 1906, the privately owned Seattle Park Company approached West Seattle's city council with a plan for an amusement park along the bathing beach at Alki. The city council approved the project, which had been named Luna Park. In January 1907, the company entered into a contract

with Charles I.D. Looff, a well-known showman and carousel carver. Looff had finished a carousel for a park in San Francisco, but after the 1906 earthquake, he needed a new location. Luna Park was an ideal setting for Looff—a waterfront site just off a streetcar line. (Author's collection.)

At the turn of the 20th century, beach bathers swarmed Alki during the summer months. The shallow shoreline was optimal for the contemporary pastime, and the receding tide revealed a wide breadth of sand. On its most populated days, thousands of beachgoers splashed in the waves at Alki. (Courtesy of Museum of History and Industry, SHS 15522.)

Alki was lined with encampments, tents, and cabins. Some were intended as summer dwellings, such as the one pictured here, and others were year-round homes. Families were raised on the beach, where life was different than it was across the bay. Wildlife, accustomed to roaming the woodlands of West Seattle, often foraged in these camps. (Courtesy of PEMCO Webster and Stevens Collection, Museum of History and Industry, 1983.10.7366.2.)

This 1907 photograph is one of the earliest taken of Luna Park. Many of its signs, including the one above the main entrance, had yet to be completed. The heart above the gate is not painted, nor is the lettering on the Canals of Venice seen in the background. Also absent are the numerous banners and world flags that flew from the minarets. (Courtesy of Dan Kerlee.)

This photograph, taken in 1907, shows the uncompleted interior of Luna Park; the bear cage and bandstand had yet to be built. Alki had hosted other vendors, but none had matched the immensity of Luna Park. The park occupied a 36-acre parcel of beach and represented an overall investment of $500,000. (Courtesy of Dan Kerlee.)

Though Luna Park's main structures were mostly built of plywood, as was customary, the overall scheme was undertaken with a high level of detail. The park featured lavish trimmings, such as the minarets around the pillars of the main gate. The crest dominating the park's entrance featured the Roman goddess Luna cradled in a crescent moon. (Author's collection.)

Built over Elliott Bay, Luna Park jutted from the northern tip of Alki. It was compared to the amusement parks at New York's Coney Island, one of which was also named Luna Park. Seattle's Luna Park was dubbed "Seattle's Coney Island," "Coney Island of Puget Sound," and "Coney Island across the Bay." Luna Park's pier, with the tide in, was a veritable East Coast boardwalk (below). (Above, courtesy of Alan Peterson; below, courtesy of Southwest Seattle Historical Society/Log House Museum.)

Luna Park opened its gates at 7:00 in the evening on June 27, 1907. Thousands arrived to get a look at the peculiar structure that, for six months, had captured their curiosity. What they found was a mechanized wonderland bathed in electric light. Luna Park was aglow and teeming with thousands of visitors late into the night. It was one of the largest crowds the park ever witnessed. This photograph includes the inside of the park's entrance and the Seattle Electric Company's Luna Park trolley stopped out front. (Courtesy of Museum of History and Industry, SHS 7792.)

Charles I.D. Looff managed the park's rides, sideshows, and games of chance. He installed an assortment of amusements, including a beautiful hand-carved carousel finished in his Rhode Island shop. The park's interior, as seen from the nearby hillside, is shown in this image. The hippodrome for Looff's carousel is visible at the bottom right, just in front of the Shoot-the-Chutes. (Courtesy of Southwest Seattle Historical Society/Log House Museum.)

The Seattle Park Company managed the park's natatorium, dance hall, barroom, and the Luna Park Café, a 600-seat restaurant. This photograph, taken from Elliott Bay on the west side of the park, includes the natatorium to the right, the café in the middle, and the dance hall to the left. (Courtesy of PEMCO Webster and Stevens Collection, Museum of History and Industry, 1983.10.9066.)

The first Luna Park, pictured at left, was located at Coney Island. In 1903, two showmen leased the aging Sea Lion Park, renovated it, and opened it under the new name. Whether or not Seattle's Luna Park, pictured below, was named in homage to Coney Island's park is unknown, but their designs have many similarities. Both amusement parks were painted white and brilliantly lit, and both featured prominent entrances that included hearts above the gates. (Left, author's collection; below, courtesy of Special Collections, University of Washington Libraries, UW 29405z.)

Other Luna Parks operated during this period but were not affiliated with the park in Seattle. Frederick Ingersoll, an inventor and amusement-park entrepreneur, opened a string of these parks across the country. In 1905, he opened a Luna Park in Pittsburgh, Pennsylvania. Shortly after, he opened one in Cleveland, Ohio. The designs of the gates differed from that of Seattle's only slightly, substituting crescent moons for a heart. (Both, author's collection.)

Entrance to Luna Park.                                    Cleveland, Ohio.

The *City of Seattle*, Puget Sound's first ferryboat, began service in 1888. The vessel was 121 feet long, 33 feet wide, and vehicles could be loaded at either end. The steam-powered ship was essential to West Seattle's real estate development, offering direct service from the Marion Street dock in Seattle to the landing at Louisiana Street in West Seattle (pictured below). (Above, courtesy of Special Collections, University of Washington Libraries, La Roche 173; below, courtesy of Puget Sound Maritime Historical Society, PSMHS 557-3.)

On Luna Park's opening day, a new ferryboat was launched on the route between the cities. Named the *West Seattle*, the ferry alternated with the *City of Seattle* to offer service across Elliott Bay. Between the two vessels, service from either side ran every 30 minutes. The new ferry was larger and more modern than the *City of Seattle*, providing two spacious passenger decks. (Courtesy of Dan Kerlee.)

The year 1907 was profitable for Seattle's ferry system. In July alone, over 100,000 passengers were ferried across the bay. Soon, the *West Seattle*, pictured at the Louisiana Street landing, handled most of the traffic. The *City of Seattle* began traveling directly to the Luna Park pleasure pier. (Courtesy of Puget Sound Maritime Historical Society, PSMHS 1741-143.)

Luna Park's opening day also marked the inaugural trip of the Seattle Electric Company's Luna Park line, which ran between downtown Seattle and West Seattle. The streetcar, like the ferry, traveled directly to the park. It stopped right in front of Luna Park's entrance, as touted in most of the park's advertisements. (Courtesy of Dan Kerlee.)

Electric streetcars, such as the Seattle Electric Railway Company car pictured above, began running in Seattle in 1889. A dependable streetcar route, running directly from West Seattle to Seattle, was first promised in 1899 but did not immediately materialize. When the Luna Park line was established, it was a boon for West Seattle's real estate. In the image below, the trolley is heading along the beach southwest of Luna Park after its route had been extended to Alki Point. (Above, courtesy of Museum of History and Industry, SHS 7704; below, courtesy of PEMCO Webster and Stevens Collection, Museum of History and Industry, 1983.10.7978.)

The Luna Park line left downtown Seattle and traveled over the tideflats by way of a bridge on Spokane Street, where the West Seattle Bridge stands today. The line then crossed a trestle over present-day Harbor Avenue and continued to the gate of Luna Park. Pictured is the route the Luna Park line traveled over the tideflats in the days before Harbor Island. (Courtesy of Museum of History and Industry, SHS 666.)

When the line was extended to Alki Point in 1908, its name was changed to the Alki Point line. The cars were equipped with signs reflecting the new name, but the Luna Park sign was still hung on the front. An advertisement reading, "At Luna Park Today" was affixed to the streetcar's cowcatcher. (Courtesy of Southwest Seattle Historical Society/Log House Museum.)

Common features of fairs and carnivals, midways were lined with concessions, games, and exhibits. The term is derived from Chicago's Columbian Exposition, which concentrated these amusements on the city's Midway Plaisance. It was the first world's fair to feature such concessions entirely apart from the exhibit halls. The first amusement park to include a midway was Coney Island's Luna Park, influencing the design of subsequent parks. In the above photograph of Seattle's Luna Park, the sandwich board advertises "LaSousa's Minstrel Band" and "Madame Schelle Taming Lions," both of which were features during the 1909 season. In the photograph below, two members of LaSousa's Minstrel Band, also advertised as LaSousa's Clown Band, can be seen at the bottom right. (Both, courtesy of Museum of History and Industry, SHS 7806, SHS 7802.)

A 10¢ admission was charged at the park's gate. This fee allowed visitors access to the midway, natatorium, café, and exhibits. The rides and concessions carried an additional charge. Pictured is Luna Park's midway with the chutes, the Canals of Venice, and the oscillating swing in the background. (Courtesy of Special Collections, University of Washington Libraries, UW 11488.)

Luna Park's display of electric lights is pictured here. It was reported that Charles I.D. Looff's intent was to make the park as light at night as it was during the day. He installed a Parsons turbine and generator and outfitted the park with about 11,000 incandescent lightbulbs. It was a stunning spectacle, and at the time, this was the city's highest concentration of electric lights. Every building at Luna Park was outlined with bulbs. Even the cars and cables of the oscillating swing were ornamented with lights. Luna Park, with its brilliant illumination, was advertised as a safe nighttime attraction for women and children. (Courtesy of Museum of History and Industry, SHS 7796.)

Nighttime illumination has been a standard feature of amusement parks, which evolved from pleasure gardens, since the 18th century. Thousands of oil lamps were once used to light these gardens, a novelty to people accustomed to dim candlelight. By the 20th century, electricity had drastically changed nighttime displays. Luna Park glowed in a mesmerizing display visible for miles at night. (Above, courtesy of Museum of History and Industry, SHS 7800; below, author's collection.)

SEATTLE AT NIGHT, FROM WEST SEATTLE, SHOWING LUNA PARK. S. S. KENNEDY AND QUEEN ANNE HILL IN THE DISTANCE

Luna Park was surrounded by a bathing beach, capitalizing on Alki's shallow coastline. Here, swimmers near Luna Park are decked out in the beach attire of the day. When swimmers tired of the icy bay, the natatorium provided heated saltwater. (Above, courtesy of Special Collections, University of Washington Libraries, UW 1123; below, courtesy of Southwest Seattle Historical Society/Log House Museum.)

Fire has long been an enemy of amusement parks, as plywood construction allowed flames to spread quickly. By the time firefighters arrived, the damage had usually been done. One night in July 1908, Luna Park nearly suffered this fate. A fire broke out along the waterfront, threatening to spread to the park. The captain of the steamer *Lydia Thompson* ordered the ship's hose unreeled, concentrating a stream of saltwater on the blaze. The night watchman from the nearby King and Winge shipyard, pictured below, did the same. Within a short time, the fire was extinguished. (Both, courtesy of Puget Sound Maritime Historical Society, PSMHS 1466-7, PSMHS 3909-1.)

Its ornamental features made Luna Park an appealing venue for social events. Church groups, businesses, and families could purchase special accommodations at the park. In September 1907, a wedding was held at Luna Park, and the entire city was invited. The couple took their vows in view of the public, and the Fort Lawton Military Band serenaded them. Another couple wed at Luna Park in 1909, holding the ceremony in the lions' cage with the animals present. The bride took a lot of convincing. (Author's collection.)

_H.P.Christofferson 1912_

AMOUS "OREGON KID," champion motor boat of the Pacific Coast, racing with Christofferson in his hydro-aeroplane at Lake Washington, near Seattle.

In 1913, aviator Harry Christofferson flew his "hydro-aeroplane," pictured here in 1912, from Everett to Seattle. He had contracted with Luna Park to place his craft on exhibit. When he and his plane arrived, Bertha Mack, a young cashier at the park, talked him into taking her for a joyride. When the young aviator agreed, Bertha Mack became the first woman to fly over Seattle. The engagement of the two soon followed. They held the ceremony at Luna Park, leaving for their honeymoon in Christofferson's plane. (Courtesy of Seattle Museum of Flight.)

# Two

# THE NATION'S GREATEST PLAYGROUND ON THE PACIFIC COAST

Seattle's Luna Park offered a sprawling midway lined with innovative diversions. Some were immense, such as the Great Figure-Eight Roller Coaster, Shoot-the-Chutes, and the oscillating swing, which would whisk visitors away at thrilling speeds. Other attractions, including the Canals of Venice and A Day in the Alps, showcased elegant murals and scenery. Luna Park's hippodrome housed a carousel featuring four rows of beautifully hand-carved figures.

The midway was home to a number of technologically advanced exhibits. The Electrical Theatre presented silent films, and the Infant Electrobator demonstrated how technology could aid in the care of premature babies. Visitors could have their photographs taken against amusing backdrops and printed onto souvenir postcards. The midway also offered games of chance, including ball tosses and a shooting gallery, in addition to exhibiting wild animals.

Charles I.D. Looff hired performers and entertainers of all varieties and presented a new act almost every week. There were high divers, jugglers, fortune-tellers, balloonists, and clowns. Luna Park also hosted such exhibits as Chinese warships and the wagon Ezra Meeker drove from Puyallup to Washington, DC. With all of its offerings, Luna Park was fittingly advertised as "The Nation's Greatest Playground on the Pacific Coast."

Luna Park offered many of the most popular amusements of the day. The park's crown jewel was its carousel, housed in the hippodrome seen to the left in this photograph. Shoot-the-Chutes, consisting of the ramp and pool pictured at center, was one of the first water rides ever devised. The oscillating swing, at the right, was a state-of-the-art ride, and the Canals of Venice behind it was synonymous with romance. (Author's collection.)

The hippodrome housed a spectacular Coney Island–style carousel with a menagerie of figures carved by Charles I.D. Looff. In addition to its horses, the carousel featured giraffes, camels, rams, and a tiger. It was Luna Park's most celebrated ride, and it was enjoyed by both adults and children. (Author's collection.)

The carousel's band organ can be seen to the left in this photograph. Its crest reads, "Chas Looff, Brooklyn, NY." Though the machine was completed in Looff's workshop at Crescent Park in Rhode Island, it is probable that work on the carousel began while his shop was still in Brooklyn, New York. (Courtesy of Museum of History and Industry, SHS 7791.)

This photograph of Luna Park's carousel exemplifies the ornate Coney Island style. The frame was adorned with hand-carved trappings, crowned with the starburst pattern that was one of Looff's trademarks, and fitted with a dazzling array of lights and mirrors. The Coney Island was the most lavish and fantastic of the carousel styles, deriving its name from the famed East Coast resort whose first carousel was crafted by Looff. (Courtesy of Museum of History and Industry, SHS 7878.)

The figures for Luna Park's carousel were carved from Japanese white pine and had tails of real horsehair. Looff also set starburst-patterned, cut-glass jewels in their trappings. He had them imported from Czechoslovakia, the only carousel carver to do so, and affixed them directly to the raw wood. This photograph illustrates one of Looff's innovations, which was to suspend figures from their poles with all four hooves in the air. (Courtesy of PEMCO Webster and Stevens Collection, Museum of History and Industry, 1983.10.7883.)

GREAT FIGURE   GREAT COASTER

Likely designed by Charles I.D. Looff's son Arthur, Luna Park's Great Figure-Eight Roller Coaster was second only to the carousel in popularity. A chain elevator drew the cars up the incline of the multilevel track. Starting from high above the midway, passengers made three laps before slowing to a halt at the bottom. (Author's collection.)

*1198  The Figure Eight Luna Park Seattle*

Luna Park's roller coaster was built on a timber frame, which would creak under the weight of the cars. Roller coasters date back to a winter amusement in Russia, where giant slides were built that would then cover over with snow. Many of the ride's innovations occurred in France, however. Because the country experienced less snowfall than Russia, the ride evolved to use cars, which ran on straight, undulating tracks. The roller coaster first appeared in the United States in the 1870s, followed by the introduction of the oval track in 1884. (Author's collection.)

The next major advance in coasters was the figure-eight configuration, such as the track at Luna Park, which had an average cost of $16,000. The figure-eight roller coaster reached the peak of its popularity around the turn of the 20th century. The cars, outfitted with four caster wheels, were guided along the track by side-friction wheels. They were powered down the track by gravity and then hoisted back to the top with a new group of passengers. While a novelty and thrill for pleasure seekers, these figure-eight coasters rarely exceeded speeds of six miles per hour. (Courtesy of PEMCO Webster and Stevens Collection, Museum of History and Industry, 1983.10.7884.)

Shoot-the-Chutes was first installed at Coney Island's Sea Lion Park in 1889. On Luna Park's Shoot-the-Chutes, passengers had a wonderful, though brief, view of the midway and Elliott Bay before barreling down the 200-foot track. Unlike modern water rides, the track for Shoot-the-Chutes ended before the lagoon began, leaving passengers to the whims of physics when hitting the water. (Courtesy of Southwest Seattle Historical Society, Log House Museum.)

Shoot-the-Chutes
evolved from water
rides built in France
during the early
1800s. Variations were
developed in America
75 years later, but
Shoot-the-Chutes
was the first to enjoy
success. In these
photographs of Luna
Park's ride, a gondola
is pictured planing
over the water. At the
bottom of the ramp,
the track curved
upward, propelling
the boat into the air
before it landed. The
boat skimmed over
the water's surface,
jostling and spraying
the passengers.
(Both, courtesy of
Museum of History
and Industry, SHS
7795, SHS 7815A.)

Oscillating swings were another amusement-park staple. The swing at Luna Park was referred to by many names, including the giant whirl, the giant swing, and the circle swing. The swing featured at Luna Park was from a design by H.E. Traver and R.S. Uzzell. The pair installed their first swing, known as the Traver Swing, at a Colorado park in 1904. (Courtesy of Dan Kerlee.)

Six cars were suspended from radial arms extending from the main tower. An engine housed in the tower turned the arms at high speeds, swinging the cars outward in a wide circle. More than 80 of these swings were built throughout the country between 1904 and 1907. They cost from $7,000 to $15,000. (Author's collection.)

The Canals of Venice, pictured above, was Luna Park's other water ride. Passengers floated in gondolas through a serpentine canal, moving past elaborately decorated scenes of Venice that included cityscapes, the countryside, and cathedrals, such as the one pictured below. The ride itself dates back to 1891, and variations of it can be found to this day. The most commonly known is the Tunnel of Love. The original ride called for numerous propellers along the canal to keep the flow of water steady. In 1902, an improved version was introduced, replacing the propellers with a large paddle wheel at one end. This simpler apparatus was most likely used at Luna Park. (Both, courtesy of Museum of History and Industry, SHS 7798, SHS 7801.)

In 1909, Luna Park added a new ride. The Joy Wheel, seen at the top left, delivered thrills by means of centrifugal force. Pleasure seekers sat on its flat circular platform. The platform spun rapidly until the last of the passengers had been ejected. Cushions surrounded the platform to catch them. It was a simple yet widely enjoyed attraction. (Courtesy of Museum of History and Industry, SHS 7814.)

To keep a hold on the public's interest, amusement parks often exhibited advanced technologies. One such concession, the Electrical Theatre, was an early form of movie theater. Pictured at Luna Park, the theater was a common feature at amusement parks of this era. Silent films were shown as pianists played the scores. (Courtesy of Museum of History and Industry, SHS 7875.)

Luna Park's natatorium was one of the few indoor swimming facilities in Seattle. It housed three pools (two saltwater and one fresh) and had room for 1,000 bathers. The saltwater pools were heated and fed directly from Elliott Bay, the water recycling at a rate of 10,000 gallons each hour. (Courtesy of Dan Kerlee.)

# ALKI POINT NATATORIUM
### SEATTLE

The Largest Swimming Tank in the Northwest
## HOT SALT WATER ——— AND ——— SURF BATHING
### Take Alki Point Car at Pioneer Square

Luna Park's was not the first natatorium in Seattle. The Alki Point Transportation Company had built Alki Point Natatorium, which included a saltwater pool, in 1905. It was quite successful its first (and possibly only) year of operation. The company planned a larger building designed in a Japanese motif, allegedly including geishas, but it was never built. The natatorium's end remains a mystery. (Author's collection.)

Luna Park's natatorium had a vast interior with a second-floor gallery for spectators. Swimmers could shoot down the slide from the second floor into the water below. A trapeze swing hung over the main pool. While the beach at Alki was already a well-known destination for bathing, the natatorium offered a more controlled environment where swimmers could receive instruction. (Courtesy of Dan Kerlee.)

The natatorium presented new opportunities for athleticism. Shortly after opening, it hosted a water carnival that included swimming races, diving contests, water polo, and obstacle races. It was credited with being the first event of its kind in Seattle. Spread over four days, the carnival drew participants from across the Northwest and as far away as Vancouver, British Columbia. The natatorium was also widely advertised to the public. This advertisement appeared in a 1909 program from the Moore Theater. (Right, author's collection; below, courtesy of Special Collections, University of Washington Libraries, UW 29312z.)

## FRESH SALT WATER

Whether the day be warm or cold

It doesn't matter, for young or old

Can take a warm salt-water swim,

Which keeps them healthy and in good trim,

At that bathing pavilion (above the mark).

**"The Natatorium,"** Luna Park.

SHE'S MAKIN A HOG OF HERSELF

Uncle Hiram, pictured with Betsy the pig, one of his sidekicks, was a recurring performer at Luna Park. His real name was Carl Hinckley, and he was a young vaudeville performer known around Seattle. He took the persona of Uncle Hiram from the hit song "Hiram Green, Good Bye," which he used to sing at the Star Theater. Already having a reputation as a "silly kid," Hinckley dressed for his new role with great detail. (Both, courtesy of Dan Kerlee.)

Hinckley paraded animals around the boardwalk to the amusement of onlookers. One of his props was this Studebaker wagon, which he hitched to novelty motorcars, as well as animals. When Hinckley left Luna Park to perform at the Western Washington Fair, he also had to leave behind Betsy. The pig was the property of Luna Park but had outgrown her role as the park's cute piglet. Unwilling to let Betsy face the chopping block, Hinckley purchased her from Charles I.D. Looff and had her transported to the fairgrounds. (Both, courtesy of Dan Kerlee.)

5. Shoeing the Oxen, Seattle, 1906.

In 1906, Ezra Meeker, founder of the city of Puyallup, Washington, drove his ox team and prairie schooner (covered wagon) from his home to Washington, DC. Meeker, seen above having one of his team shoed for his 1906 expedition, had journeyed the trail as a young man, traveling with his family from Ohio to the Pacific Northwest. Aiming to draw national attention to the preservation of the Oregon Trail, Meeker hitched up his oxen, Dave and Dandy, and set out on this highly publicized trek. (Above, author's collection; below, courtesy of Dan Kerlee.)

RA MEEKER AT LUNA PARK SEATTLE AFTER A 3650 MILE TRIP WITH AN OX TEAM

Meeker stopped frequently to promote the trip, charging admission to view his wagon. He also built about 20 modest markers along the trail, a number he hoped to increase to 500 or 600 with funds from Congress. Meeker reached New York City in the fall of 1907 and drove his team along the streets, lecturing about the Oregon Trail. He continued on to Washington, DC, and met with Pres. Theodore Roosevelt. Meeker returned to Seattle with his team in 1908, making a string of publicity appearances that included Luna Park. Meeker traveled the Oregon Trail for the final time in 1924, flying from Washington to Ohio in a US Army airplane. He was 94 years old. (Author's collection.)

Balloon ascensions, such as this one at Luna Park, were a draw for amusement parks around the turn of the 20th century. Ballooning dates back to the late 18th century, but numerous accidents caused performers to abandon the practice. In 1887, Thomas Scott Baldwin reintroduced it. The date of the photograph above corresponds with advertisements for balloonist M.E. Davidson. The postcard below depicts the balloon tied down on the midway. Davidson performed at the park for about a week, making an ascension each afternoon at 3:00. (Both, author's collection.)

Ballooning was a frequent showpiece at Luna Park. The park owned this balloon and used it for ascensions, sometimes with the aeronaut vying to set records for altitude. Balloon races were also held between aeronauts. In July 1909, Luna Park's balloon was carried off by the wind and snagged at the top of a 100-foot-tall cedar. It took expert climbers almost a week to retrieve it. (Courtesy of Dan Kerlee.)

During the Alaska-Yukon-Pacific Exposition in 1909, Luna Park's balloon was loaned out for the occasion. It was primarily used to give ascension rides to fairgoers. Here, the Luna Park balloon floats above the Canada Building at the fairgrounds. (Courtesy of Special Collections, University of Washington Libraries, UW 20407z.)

Luna Park, Seattle, Wash.

TEDDY TAKING A DRINK IN SEATTLE

Charles I.D. Looff loved featuring animals at his parks. Here, a collection of dogs and ponies pose at Luna Park, and a curious bear peers through the bars behind them. The animals might have belonged to Looff. Many of his figures (or "steeds," as he called them) featured monkeys riding on their backs, much like the monkey atop the pony in the photograph. An act billed as a trained monkey and dog circus also appeared at the park. (Courtesy of Southwest Seattle Historical Society/Log House Museum.)

The bears on display at Luna Park were actually Looff's personal pets. In this photograph, he is feeding one of his bear cubs from a bottle. Though the bear pit's cage protected visitors from the bears, it did not always work the other way around. In 1909, one of the bears died when a visitor fed it poisoned candy through the bars. (Courtesy of Museum of History and Industry, SHS 7804.)

High divers were standard spectacle at amusement parks and carnivals, leaping from great heights into tanks just a few feet deep. Several high-diving acts passed through Luna Park, having monikers like "Spray." The diver pictured here is most likely Diavlo, who appeared at Luna Park in the summer of 1908. He dived from 120 feet, setting his tank ablaze at night for a more daring spectacle. He was hospitalized after undertaking this stunt and had to cancel several performances. (Right, courtesy of PEMCO Webster and Stevens Collection, Museum of History and Industry, 1983.10.7886; below, courtesy of Museum of History and Industry, SHS 7704.)

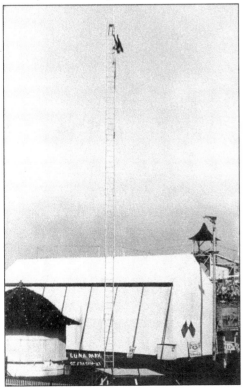

Charles I.D. Looff hired new acts almost weekly. Visitors to Luna Park were treated to the antics of sideshow daredevils who were increasingly elaborate in their devices. In the photograph at left, a duo performs acrobatic bicycle stunts. They might be the Great Martells, who were advertised as champion trick cyclists. The photograph below shows a performer landing at the end of a rope slide. The man might be Charles Leora. He would start at a height of 80 feet and slide down a 700-foot cable while hanging by his teeth. He called the stunt Slide for Life. (Left, courtesy of PEMCO Webster and Stevens Collection, Museum of History and Industry, 1983.10.7885; below, courtesy of Museum of History and Industry, SHS 7793.)

A MONSTROUS 100 TON PORT ANGELES WHALE
ON EXHIBITION AT LUNA PARK
DEC. 30TH 1907

Taking advantage of Luna Park's proximity to the bay, Charles I.D. Looff frequently exhibited whale carcasses off the end of the pier. The above postcard commemorates one such exhibit. Looff made arrangements with whaling companies to purchase the mammals for display. In 1908, an orca whale was caught in a fish trap in Anacortes and had to be killed. Looff had it towed to Luna Park. (Author's collection.)

During its first season, Luna Park exhibited the Chinese war junk *Whang Ho*, an infamous pirate-hunting vessel. The ship was advertised as having been built with "beautiful and costly Oriental woods" and inlaid with genuine pearl. Also on exhibit were the ship's extensive arsenal of weapons and instruments of torture. (Courtesy of www.flickr.com/photos/china-postcard.)

Bandstands were common at amusement parks. They featured live musical performances and were designed for large audiences. Luna Park's first bandstand, pictured above in 1907, showcased a number of ensembles. Sometimes, vocalists sang along with the park's orchestrion. In the photograph below, a brass band performs for a sizable audience. (Both, courtesy of Museum of History and Industry, SHS 7815B, SHS 7812.)

In 1908, during off-season renovations, a shell-shaped bandstand was added to Luna Park. It offered better acoustics than its predecessor and presented musical performances in a setting more like a stage. The bandstand, with its awning standing to shade the audience, is pictured. (Courtesy of Museum of History and Industry, SHS 7811.)

Vaudeville was one of the most popular forms of entertainment in Luna Park's day. It encompassed a variety of acts ranging from animal trainers to vocalists. The acts were performed in small theaters, another standard feature of amusement parks. Performers of all kinds graced the stage of Luna Park's Trocadero Theatre. The act advertised here is for Mantell's Marionette Hippodrome. (Courtesy of Dan Kerlee.)

The Kuhn brothers, pictured here in 1903, were vaudeville sensations. The trio appeared at Luna Park in 1908 with the Kuhn & Lawrence Show, which they also managed. The variety act included a trained leopard and lion, and the brothers took the stage with song numbers. (Courtesy of Special Collections, University of Washington Libraries, UW 29409z.)

Angela May was another of Luna Park's performers. A comic opera singer, May studied music abroad for two years before appearing as an entertainer. She was noted not only for possessing a powerful contralto voice but also for her spot-on impersonations. May, pictured here in a 1906 promotional portrait, gained notoriety for her compositions, as well. (Courtesy of Special Collections, University of Washington Libraries, UW 29408z.)

Seattle's Luna Park was featured in two commercial songs, one about the park itself and the other about Uncle Hiram. Pictured here is the cover for "All Aboard for Luna Park," published during the park's first season. Angela May wrote the lyrics and later performed the piece at the park. (Courtesy of Southwest Seattle Historical Society/Log House Museum.)

"Uncle Hirum at the Fair" was an homage to the clown Uncle Hiram (though spelled with a "u" in the sheet music seen at left, common usage in newspapers and at the park was always "Hiram"). Carl Hinckley, who played Hiram, was a favorite with the crowds at Luna Park, as well as at a number of fairs throughout the Northwest. In the song from which Hinckley took the character, Uncle Hiram was a rube who thought himself an aristocrat. (Courtesy of Southwest Seattle Historical Society/Log House Museum.)

At Luna Park's Magic Photograph Palace, visitors could have their image taken against a variety of backdrops. Photography had only recently progressed to film, so having a photograph taken and developed while waiting was a novel treat for visitors. The automobile, also fairly new, was a favorite prop for these souvenir photographs. (Both, author's collection.)

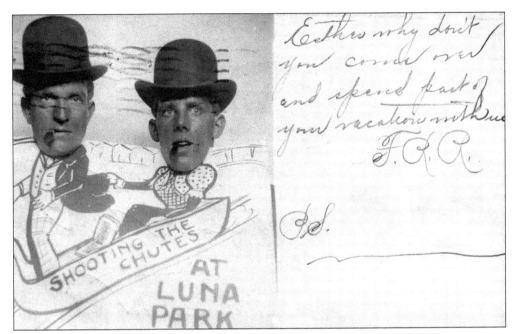

Background options also included caricatures of some of Luna Park's rides, such as the chutes seen in the postcard above. Dirigible balloons were also a popular attraction at the time, with L. Guy Mecklem's airship flight from Luna Park in 1908 and J.C. Bud Mars's craft at the Alaska-Yukon-Pacific Exposition in 1909. The dirigible made for a whimsical backdrop as well. These photographs were printed onto postcards, a form of correspondence then at the height of its popularity. (Both, author's collection.)

Attractive and inexpensive, ruby flash glass was ubiquitous around the turn of the 20th century. The glass was pressed, but the designs evolved to an intricacy nearly mimicking cut glass. Flash glass was also prevalent at fairs, amusement parks, and similar attractions, as it could be easily etched to commemorate the occasion. These pieces of flash glass were sold at Seattle's Luna Park. (Photograph by author.)

Pins were another favorite souvenir of the day. Seattle's Luna Park sold pins in these three designs. Walking arm in arm are Alphonse and Gaston, characters of a popular comic strip. Their taglines were, "After you, my dear Alphonse," and, "You first, my dear Gaston," respectively. (Photograph by author.)

# Three

# Pioneer of the Coney Island Style

In August 1870, a young immigrant arrived in New York's harbor from the province of Schleswig-Holstein. He had little wealth but possessed exceptional artistic talent and fierce ambition. Within a decade, he had established himself as a master carousel carver and the pioneer of the Coney Island style, a form so richly embellished it verged on the surreal. His name was Charles I.D. Looff.

Looff settled in Brooklyn and found work carving furniture, taking wood scraps home at night and shaping them into animals. It is not known for certain where Looff learned to carve, but it was likely in his homeland, which enjoyed a rich tradition of wood carving and carousel building. Looff might have apprenticed in a carousel factory, honing the skills that would one day advance him to the vanguard of the industry.

The Coney Island style of carving, named for the East Coast resort where Looff installed his first machine, was the most ornate and, arguably, the most artistic. Adorned with cut-glass jewels, mirrors, and other extravagant trappings, Looff's carousels were more flamboyant than the Philadelphia or country-fair styles. His figures blended stoicism with jollity, particularly the steeds, as he called them, with their gallant poses, gold-leaf manes, and laughing expressions.

At the end of his life, Charles I.D. Looff was a self-made millionaire. He had built more than 40 carousels, and his machines ran on both seaboards. Only about 12 of Looff's original machines still operate, including the one from Luna Park. Relics of the wondrous industry of hand-carved carousels, their figures attest to Looff's mastery of the craft.

*First Carousell in the U. S. at Coney Island, N.Y. 1876*

*Charles I.D. Looff*

Charles I.D. Looff built Coney Island's very first carousel in 1875. Looff, seen here with the machine in 1876, carved its figures in his apartment. It was placed on the grounds of Vandeveer's Bathing Pavilion, later sold and renamed Balmer's Pavilion. The machine had 27 figures displayed in three rows. Among them were a camel, goat, zebra, stork, and horses in standing and leaping poses. Looff's granddaughter, Willi Looff Taucher, claimed a horse was harnessed to the platform to power the machine, a practice later considered inhumane. Many years later, Looff's first carousel was offered back to him in payment for a debt. Looff, by then a wealthy man, joked he would use the machine for a watch fob. (Courtesy of the Tobin Fraley/Carousel News & Trader Archive.)

An ambitious man, Looff also taught ballroom dancing part-time while employed carving furniture. A young woman named Anna Dolle, pictured above with Charles Looff, came to the studio as a student. They were married in 1874. All of their six children, except for their daughter Anna, who died at a young age, went on to work for Looff in the amusement business. (Courtesy of Museum of History and Industry, SHS 7790.)

Looff's second carousel, commissioned by Charles Feltman for his restaurant complex, was also installed at Coney Island. While a vendor at Coney Island, Feltman sought to produce a snack with broad appeal. The result was the hot dog. By 1920, Feltman was so successful that he built a restaurant capable of serving 1,000 patrons a day. Looff, encouraged by his own success, established a workshop in Brooklyn, New York. (Courtesy of the Tobin Fraley/Carousel News & Trader Archive.)

Looff placed his third carousel at Young's Pier in Atlantic City, New Jersey. The machine was so popular that the pier's owner offered to buy it. Over the protestations of his wife, Looff took the offer. In 1905, the City of New York used eminent domain to acquire Looff's property for part of a new park. Looff relocated his workshop to Crescent Park in Riverside, Rhode Island. It was at this shop that Looff completed his first carousel for the West Coast, pictured below, which was installed at Seattle's Luna Park. (Above, courtesy of Crescent Park Archive; below, courtesy of the Tobin Fraley/Carousel News & Trader Archive.)

When Charles I.D. Looff made the trek west, he took his son William along. William, who had followed his father into the family business, took over responsibilities as Luna Park's manager when his father traveled. This photograph shows William Looff (second from the right), family members, and park employees in front of one of Luna Park's attractions, the Cave of Mystery. (Courtesy of Museum of History and Industry, SHS 7877.)

Seattle's Luna Park was Looff's first endeavor on the West Coast. The Seattle Park Company needed a manager for the park's amusements; Charles I.D. Looff had the experience, as well as a brand-new carousel. He and William invested $250,000 in the project, leasing the easterly five lots of the pleasure pier and constructing its amusement devices. (Courtesy of SWSHS/Log House Museum.)

Looff's second carousel on the West Coast was placed at Natatorium Park in Spokane, Washington, in 1909. Looff gave the carousel, pictured here, and its management to his daughter Emma and her husband as a belated wedding present. The carousel still operate at Spokane's Riverfront Park. (Courtesy of Northwest Museum of Arts & Culture/Eastern Washington State Historical Society, Spokane, Washington, L86-226.)

Charles I.D. Looff, seen here playing with his pet bear cubs at Luna Park, was a lover of animals. He included them at his attractions and hired many performers who trained them. Looff enjoyed keeping a variety of exotic animals as pets, including the badger in the photograph above. (Both, courtesy of Southwest Seattle Historical Society/Log House Museum.)

Looff often included a variety of animals in his carousels. In the above photograph of the carousel from Luna Park, a monkey sits on the back of one of the steeds. This monkey was a hallmark of many of Looff's carousel figures. (Photograph by David H.M. Spector.)

Other Looff figures, such as this cherub from Luna Park's carousel, underscored his penchant for whimsy. Gnomes, griffins, and other fantastical creatures could often be seen peering out from the extravagant trappings of Looff's figures. (Photograph by Tim Wrye.)

Looff's youngest son, Arthur, pictured here with Charles and Anna Dolle Looff, was known as a mechanical genius. He left school in the eighth grade to work for his father. He later earned a degree in civil engineering and designed buildings and amusements, including some of those at Seattle's Luna Park. (Courtesy of Crescent Park Archive.)

In 1910, Charles Looff moved his family, home, and workshop from Riverside to The Pike, a pleasure pier in Long Beach, California. Looff also established his largest carousel factory in Long Beach, where he carved the carousel exhibited in the 1915 Panama Pacific International Exposition. (Author's collection.)

Looff installed this hippodrome, a four-row machine composed entirely of horses, at The Pike. He also built a two-bedroom apartment on the second floor, which he and his wife occupied. He lived his last days in that apartment, the band organ and laughter sounding faintly through the floor. He died of cancer on July 1, 1918, his wife at his side. She, too, lived out her days above the carousel. (Courtesy of the Tobin Fraley/Carousel News & Trader Archive.)

The family business, Looff's Amusements, passed to Arthur. He moved the carousel to a vacant building nearby and installed a Lite-A-Line in the hippodrome. The carousel burned in July 1943, a common end for the old wooden machines. Surveying the wreckage of his father's work, Arthur said, "Well, that's gone. Let's go get some breakfast." (Author's collection.)

# Four

# THE WILD SCOTSMAN

In the spring of 1897, Leschi Park's aeronaut suffered serious burns while inflating his gas balloon. Volunteering to take his place was 15-year-old Llewellyn Guy Mecklem, a small-framed high-school dropout who worked in Leschi's boathouse. He ascended from Leschi, but the parachute refused to detach. The balloon at last cooled, dropped, and crashed into the frigid waters of Lake Washington.

It was Mecklem's first balloon ascension. In spite of its failure, he took over the aeronaut's contract and was given a $10 bonus to return the following season. Flight entranced the young man, as did attention and applause. Regardless of its inherent dangers, he was determined to make a career of it. It was a calling that would see Mecklem pilot Seattle's first manned flight.

Over the next couple of years, Mecklem performed ascensions in a balloon of his own design, establishing himself as a daredevil and earning the nickname "Wild Scotsman." This reputation came at the price of numerous calamities, including a broken knee and dislocated wrists. Mecklem abandoned this career several times because of discouragement and sometimes injury, but he always came back to it.

Riveted by Santos Dumont's 1901 dirigible flight around the Eiffel Tower, Mecklem aspired to design, build, and pilot his own airship. He rented a hall in south Seattle, ordered the materials, and set to work. In the winter of 1907, Mecklem approached Charles I.D. Looff about exhibiting his dirigible. That summer, Mecklem's airship drew thousands to Luna Park.

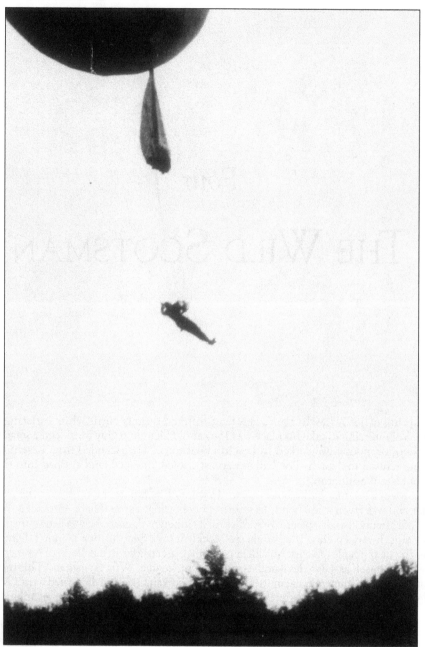

L. Guy Mecklem, pictured here around 1902, attended night school to gain the skills necessary to create his first balloon. The parachute hung below the balloon by a rope, which ran through a mechanism called a cut-off block. When Mecklem wanted to detach it, a tug sent the block's razor through the rope and freed the parachute. Aeronauts hung from their chutes by trapeze bars and from there performed stunts. Inspired by circus acts, Mecklem once devised a leather mouthpiece for his trapeze and performed ascensions hanging by his teeth. Aeronauts had little influence over where they, let alone their balloons, landed. Mecklem had to be fished out of rivers, recovered from orchards, and he was sometimes held accountable for property damage. (Courtesy of L. Guy Mecklem Collection, Center for Pacific Northwest Studies, Western Washington University, 001.)

Mecklem's balloon wore out, and its replacement ripped on its first ascension. He crashed in a chicken yard and did not bother retrieving the balloon. In 1903, he took over for a balloonist at Chutes Park in Los Angeles, performing what he called "the Human Meteor" at nighttime. He sewed a pad of asbestos to his shirt, soaked it in gasoline, and then ignited it while riding a bicycle down the chutes. The next summer, Mecklem ascended from the beach resorts of Playa del Rey, Santa Monica, and Venice, pictured in the postcard below. (Both, author's collection.)

While Mecklem was touring in the north, Capt. Thomas Scott Baldwin arrived at Chutes Park. Baldwin was famous for building the *California Arrow*, considered America's first successful airship. Baldwin was too heavy for the new airship he was exhibiting, and his protégé had recently quit to build his own airships. (Author's collection.)

When Mecklem returned to Chutes Park in need of a job, Baldwin hired him, and the two set to work with this peculiar craft. Mounted to the kayak-shaped car were two bamboo rods capped with silk paddles—oars to guide the ship through the air. It took Mecklem weeks of practice to master it. (Courtesy of L. Guy Mecklem Collection, Center for Pacific Northwest Studies, Western Washington University, 013.)

Mecklem was no closer to building his own craft. When the oar-powered dirigible mysteriously exploded, Mecklem left Chutes Park. He returned to Seattle during the summer of 1906 and joined the Northwest Auto Track Association, exchanging ballooning for racing. For the next two seasons, he toured around the state racing a Franklin Spider (he is posing with it in this photograph). When the 1907 season concluded, Mecklem returned his attention skyward. (Courtesy of the *Seattle Times*.)

Mecklem rented Newell's Hall in South Seattle. He ordered 360 yards of Japanese silk to sew the gasbag, which measured 58 feet in length. Fish netting was used to help secure the framework below. The framework itself was held together with T-bolts and strengthened with 200-pound-test piano wire. (Courtesy of L. Guy Mecklem Collection, Center for Pacific Northwest Studies, Western Washington University, 021.)

Mecklem moved the completed airship to Luna Park in June 1908, housing it in the specially constructed hangar seen to the left of the roller coaster. The hangar measured 70 feet in length and 30 in width, large enough to house the spindle-shaped craft with room for maintenance. The temporary structure was built in just two days. (Above, author's collection; below, courtesy of Dan Kerlee.)

The dirigible's air-cooled, two-cylinder engine sputtered at an output of 10 horsepower. Mecklem added a friction cone clutch, which he claimed had only been employed on zeppelins to that point. With the clutch, Mecklem could disengage the propeller and bring the craft to a standstill in midair. All of the craft's components fit into two trunks, which together weighed less than 500 pounds. (Courtesy of L. Guy Mecklem Collection, Center for Pacific Northwest Studies, Western Washington University, 009.)

Inflating the gasbag required about 2,000 gallons of sulfuric acid, 2,500 pounds of cast-iron shavings, 300 pounds of ice, and a barrel of lime. The resulting hydrogen gas was generated with this plant, which Mecklem built using carbon-lined wine barrels. (Courtesy of L. Guy Mecklem Collection, Center for Pacific Northwest Studies, Western Washington University, 023.)

FIRST AIRSHIP ASCENSION IN SEATTLE
LUNA PARK

A test flight was scheduled for June 27, 1908. It was burdened by mishaps from the start. The barrels of acid Mecklem ordered crashed through the pier's planking on delivery. It took four days to retrieve them from the muck below. Then, one night, the plant's barrels began to jerk violently. Afraid they were about to burst, Mecklem knocked out their safety corks, showering himself with hot acid. He dived from the pier, the saltwater doing nothing for his burns. He continued filling the gasbag as he recovered, intent on his ship's debut. An eager crowd gathered at Luna Park as Mecklem's craft hovered above the boardwalk. Mecklem climbed in and told the men holding the ropes, "Let her go." (Courtesy of L. Guy Mecklem Collection, Center for Pacific Northwest Studies, Western Washington University, 017.)

The airship rose too rapidly. The gasbag distended and burst, leaving a five-foot slit along the bottom. Mecklem pulled the silk together, punctured eyelets with his jackknife, and sewed the bag back up. With the loss of gas, the airship dropped. The framework landed in Elliott Bay but remained mostly intact, the remaining gas having softened its landing. Mecklem himself suffered only wet feet. Had the bag torn at the top of the balloon, Mecklem could not have sewn it, and the ship would have hit the water like a rock. (Courtesy of L. Guy Mecklem Collection, Center for Pacific Northwest Studies, Western Washington University, 013.)

Mecklem, at left with his airship, claimed to be undiscouraged. Accidents of that sort were to be expected, he told the *Seattle Times*. He hired two seamstresses to mend the balloon (one of them is pictured below). The hydrogen fumes nauseated one of the girls; the other Mecklem eventually married. He reconstructed the framework, and a second flight was advertised for the Fourth of July. It was to be a race between Mecklem's dirigible and two Franklin automobiles. Billed as the first contest of its kind, the event drew an audience of about 12,000 to Luna Park. (Both, courtesy of L. Guy Mecklem Collection, Center for Pacific Northwest Studies, Western Washington University, 018, 010.)

On July 4, 1908, Mecklem's airship rose from Luna Park and headed south. He shouted to the drivers that he would be landing at the Meadows, a horse racetrack south of Seattle. The drivers sped through Georgetown, but Mecklem continued straight, well ahead of his competitors. Misjudging the remaining distance, he valved too much gas. The balloon dropped swiftly, heading directly for the Duwamish River. Mecklem threw all of his ballast, tools, and even his shoes overboard. The airship rose and glided just over the river, landing in a Japanese garden adjacent to the track. Mecklem and his ship were nearly mobbed by spectators. (Both, courtesy of L. Guy Mecklem Collection, Center for Pacific Northwest Studies, Western Washington University, 019, 008.)

Mecklem had piloted Seattle's first manned flight. Moreover, the Meadows was located on part of what would later become Boeing Field, making Mecklem the first to navigate its airspace. The airship was carried by a launch back to Luna Park, a dangerous trip given the fireworks along the riverbanks. Mecklem charged park visitors 10¢ to view it. In a piece for the *Seattle Times* the preceding April, he had claimed airplanes would never compete with railroads, steamships, or automobiles for carrying freight or passengers and would "never be as safe or satisfactory as the dirigible balloon." The prediction made him chuckle later in life. (Courtesy of L. Guy Mecklem Collection, Center for Pacific Northwest Studies, Western Washington University, 012.)

# Five

# THE LONGEST BAR
# ON THE BAY

When West Seattle's city council extended a saloon license to accommodate Luna Park's bar, it set the stage for a familiar conflict. The first ordinances West Seattle drafted when it incorporated in 1902 regulated the sale of alcohol, defined vagrancy and disorderly conduct, suppressed gambling, and specifically prohibited slot machines. Punishments were created, as was a jail. Citizens once ransacked a bar they thought was improperly licensed, destroying every last barrel.

Luna Park's bar was to be "the longest bar on the bay," a designation that incensed a number of West Seattle residents. The park was targeted by anti-saloon campaigns. Rumors of vice at the park began to circulate, followed by petitions to close down its bar. Citizens groups were organized, complaints were filed, and negotiations were conducted. Underage drinking was alleged, in addition to violations of Seattle's Sunday closure law. Police raids followed.

Legend attributes Luna Park's closure to the anti-saloon forces behind Seattle's first mayoral recall; it was their persistent railing against the park's alleged vice that ultimately shut the gates. This idea stems largely from an article written during the recall campaign of Hiram C. Gill and published in the *Seattle Post-Intelligencer*, which notoriously opposed him. This story is rooted in some facts and authenticated by Seattle's rampant vice conditions. However, Luna Park and its bar remained open for two years after Seattle's infamous recall election.

Luna Park concerned the citizens of West Seattle. When the Seattle Park Company approached the city council with its plan for Luna Park, they insisted it include a bar; it was a necessity if the park was to be profitable. The city council accommodated by extending the saloon limits. When West Seattle citizens discovered the plan for the bar, they were outraged. (Courtesy of PEMCO Webster and Stevens Collection, Museum of History and Industry, 1983.10.8281.2.)

West Seattle had considered annexation by Seattle several times. It would secure water, electricity, and police. Luna Park added another incentive. Youngstown, pictured above, was necessary for West Seattle's annexation but continually refused. At one election, Youngstown saloon keepers showed up armed to protect their interests. When West Seattle, whose waterfront is pictured below, finally got the vote, its city attorney immediately sped to Olympia to file the papers, reportedly to prevent Youngstown's saloon keepers from filing an injunction. West Seattle was officially annexed into the city of Seattle on July 24, 1907. It was the second largest annexation in Seattle's history. (Above, courtesy of Special Collections, University of Washington Libraries, A. Curtis 11540; below, courtesy of Dan Kerlee.)

WEST SEATTLE WATER FRONT

Luna Park, seen here from Elliott Bay, now fell under Seattle's laws, which prohibited the sale of liquor in parks. Seattle also disallowed games of chance in parks, threatening Luna Park's shooting gallery, ball tosses, and every other game awarding prizes. However, the park's managers filed suit against the city, and the state supreme court ultimately allowed these concessions. (Courtesy of Dan Kerlee.)

Luna Park also continued to run its infamous bar. In 1908, a number of West Seattle residents urged Seattle's city council to close the saloons on their side of the bay, Luna Park's among them. Seattle offered the saloon keepers a compromise: the saloons could operate uninterrupted for one more year, but then they had to close for good. Two proprietors, Seattle Park Company presumably one of them, refused. (Courtesy of Dan Kerlee.)

West Seattle citizens next circulated a petition to place a referendum revoking the Seattle Park Company's liquor license on the ballot. One week later, another petition was filed by a number of West Seattle citizens requesting their signatures be removed from the previous one. The referendum was effectively buried. Friends of Luna Park's bar might have exercised some influence over this turnabout. The park, whose midway is depicted in these postcards, continued to operate in full. (Both, author's collection.)

Hiram C. Gill, pictured here, won the Republican nomination for Seattle's 1910 mayoral race. Vice was a central issue for the city. Gill ran on an open-town platform, promising to relegate the restricted district to an area so remote it would be a chore to find. He won the election. Within months, reform organizations banded against him under the direction of the Public Welfare League. (Courtesy of Seattle Municipal Archives.)

Gill appointed Charles W. Wappenstein, pictured here at the Alaska-Yukon-Pacific Exposition in 1909, chief of police. "Wappy," as he was called, was linked to numerous scandals, but Gill, nevertheless, put him in charge of controlling the restricted district. It was a signal that Seattle was wide open. Wappy collected thousands in bribes each month from the proprietors of brothels and gambling houses. Establishments that did not pay were raided. (Courtesy of Special Collections, University of Washington Libraries, UW 27558z.)

The Largest House of Prostitution in the World, Constructed in a Public Street, Under the Sanction and Approval of H. C. Gill, when Mayor, and now Ready for Occupancy.

Liquor and gambling laws were so relaxed under the Gill administration that the city's two main vice lords formed the Hillside Improvement Company. The company's first project was a resort on Beacon Hill intended to be the hub of the new restricted district. Its main attraction was this massive brothel. (Courtesy of Special Collections, University of Washington Libraries, UW 8235.)

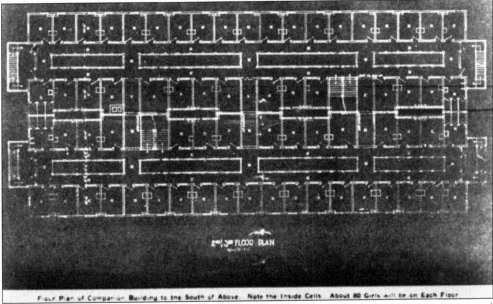

2nd, 3rd FLOOR PLAN

Floor Plan of Companion Building to the South of Above. Note the Inside Cells. About 80 Girls will be on Each Floor

The floor plan included 500 rooms, a project requiring 80 feet of a public street. The city council passed an ordinance granting the company a 15-year lease on the land. Hiram Gill signed it. With projected annual earnings of $500,000, the enterprise was considered a sound investment. However, the Public Welfare League obtained an injunction preventing its opening. (Courtesy of Special Collections, University of Washington Libraries, UW 2508.)

Under Gill, the restricted district, seen in the above 1911 photograph, continually spilled over its boundaries. The Public Welfare League circulated a petition for the recall of Mayor Gill in response. A 1906 provision in the city's charter allowed that any elected official could be removed from office by a plurality vote. It took the Public Welfare League three months to gather the necessary signatures to force a recall election. They selected George W. Dilling, pictured at left, to run against Gill. (Above, courtesy of PEMCO Webster and Stevens Collection, Museum of History and Industry, 1983.10.6784; left, courtesy of Seattle Municipal Archives.)

Luna Park was singled out in a caustic newspaper article. "Many Drunken Boys and Girls at Luna Park," read a headline in the *Seattle Post-Intelligencer*. Beer was sold all night, the article declared. Moreover, it claimed Wappenstein knew of this debauchery and placed patrolmen on detail only to prevent property damage. Police addressed underage drinking and the selling of liquor on Sundays with a wink under Wappy's leadership, according to the newspaper. The article also alleged that W.W. Powers, president of the Seattle Park Company, was an investor in the Beacon Hill brothel, as well as a contributor to Gill's campaign. (Both, author's collection.)

*1196 The Board Walk Luna Park Seattle*

*I didn't go to church here last Sunday, but the music was nice and the girl a fine dancer. Jame*

Luna Park's dance hall was also denounced in the article as luring young people astray and fostering unsavory behavior. The postcard at left is illustrative of this concern. It is inscribed, "I didn't go to church here last Sunday, but the music was nice and the girl a fine dancer." Though the bar itself, located in the park's café building (below), was closed in accordance with Seattle's Sunday closure law, the *Seattle Post-Intelligencer* alleged an automobile was used as a portable saloon. Drunken youth poured onto the ferries and trolleys, the newspaper claimed. (Both, author's collection.)

LUNA PARK CAFE AND NATORIUM
SEATTLE, U.S.A.

In 1910, Washington established voting rights for women, which changed the political atmosphere in Seattle considerably. Vice was a significant issue to the new female voters. Gill's supporters attempted to conduct the recall before these new rights were enacted, but they were unsuccessful. Dilling's supporters even established a campaign headquarters for women. Gill's supporters responded by rallying box-house girls to the polls. Dilling won the election by a comfortable lead, the majority of the nation's newspapers crediting the female vote with Gill's defeat. (Courtesy of Museum of History and Industry, SHS 5211.)

Dilling fired Wappenstein. A grand jury—having heard evidence of bribery, gambling, and other vice—sent him to the penitentiary in Walla Walla. Hiram Gill made an unsuccessful run for mayor in 1912. In 1914, he ran again, this time on a closed-town platform, and was elected. Luna Park, seen in the above photograph, continued to operate all of its concessions, including the bar. However, under the Dilling administration, frequent police raids on the bar and dance hall were carried out. The Seattle Park Company replied with a lawsuit. In the enlarged image below, a beer garden sponsored by the Rainier Brewing Company stands to the right of the dance hall. (Both, courtesy of PEMCO Webster and Stevens Collection, Museum of History and Industry, 1983.10.8281.1.)

# Six

# THE COST OF BIG AMUSEMENT

It took capital to run Luna Park. Beyond the initial investment to build it were the expenses to cover its operation. The owners had to renew annual licenses with the city for the park's concessions and pay a sizable electric bill for its illumination. There was also the park's general upkeep, advertising, and the payroll for employees. The park also needed a steady succession of performers. East Coast showman Frederick Thompson called the sum of such expenses "the cost of big amusement."

While Luna Park enjoyed immense patronage in its first seasons, punctuated with an influx of visitors during the Alaska-Yukon-Pacific Exposition, its novelty started wearing off, and its popularity declined. There was also discord between the Seattle Park Company and Charles I.D. Looff that grew contentious and ultimately played out in court. The threat of additional lawsuits loomed after an injured visitor filed a successful claim.

Luna Park also faced competition. A new civic project, Alki Beach Park, had opened near Alki Point. The new park included a natatorium with a saltwater pool, as well as a stretch of bathing beach. It later added a bandstand. Its attendance soared while Luna Park's dwindled. Charles I.D. Looff decided to cut his losses. He sold the Luna Park Amusement Company and left Seattle three years before his contract was to expire. The park, with the exception of its natatorium and dance hall, closed soon after.

By Luna Park's final season, Seattle had progressed into an industrial city. Population tripled during the first decade of the 20th century, which would seem to be to the advantage of Luna Park. The above photograph shows Elliott Bay from Beacon Hill around 1914. On the left stands

the failed Luna Park awaiting demolition. On the right stands the newly finished Smith Tower, the tallest building west of Ohio at the time. (Courtesy of PEMCO Webster and Stevens Collection, Museum of History and Industry, 1983.10.9837.2, 1983.10.9837.1.)

Luna Park's amusements were disassembled beginning in 1914. Injuries and their resulting lawsuits have always been a danger for amusement parks. In 1911, a blacksmith injured himself while swinging a mallet for the high striker, one of the park's games. The mallet's head fell off on the upstroke, and the blacksmith struck his knee instead. He claimed the injury impaired his work and sued the Luna Park Amusement Company for $10,000. He was awarded a settlement of $800. (Both, courtesy of PEMCO Webster and Stevens Collection, Museum of History and Industry, 1983.10.10291.3, 1983.10.10293.1.)

This injury was not the first to be sustained at Luna Park. In 1910, a marine engineer broke his neck on the Shoot-the-Chutes. He had ascended the ride for a better view of the park and fell head first down the track, dying two days later. While no lawsuit stemmed from the accident, the event illustrates the risk involved in operating such attractions. The ride's emptied artificial lagoon and splintered gondola are pictured here. (Courtesy of PEMCO Webster and Stevens Collection, Museum of History and Industry, 1983.10.10293.2.)

Looff, whose hippodrome is being disassembled in these photographs, filed a lawsuit of his own. He claimed the Seattle Park Company had repeatedly violated their contract by operating a number of slot machines at Luna Park. The terms of their agreement allowed Looff to run amusement devices, including games of chance. The agreement also stipulated the two companies could not offer competing attractions. (Both, courtesy of PEMCO Webster and Stevens Collection, Museum of History and Industry, 1983.10.10290, 1983.10.10292.3.)

Luna Park's main entrance, pictured being dismantled above, was also a point of conflict. Under their agreement, Looff managed the main gate and paid the Seattle Park Company a percentage of the take. But the Seattle Park Company opened a separate entrance for the natatorium, charged a reduced admission, and did not compensate Looff at all. The company even posted a billboard advertising the low fee and employed a man to point visitors toward the less expensive gate. Once inside, nothing prevented guests from continuing on to the amusements, bypassing the main gate. Looff claimed this cost him thousands of dollars. (Both, courtesy of PEMCO Webster and Stevens Collection, Museum of History and Industry, 1983.10.10292.1, 1983.10.10292.2.)

William Looff also filed a complaint against the Seattle Park Company. Both lawsuits sought permanent injunctions against the company, whose dance hall is seen in this photograph. The injunctions were denied. The court instead told the Looffs they were free to fence off their premises so long as the fence was entirely on their property. The decision displeased them. (Courtesy of PEMCO Webster and Stevens Collection, Museum of History and Industry, 1983.10.10291.2.)

The Seattle Park Company, whose Summer Garden is pictured being dismantled here, countersued Looff. The complaint claimed Looff's lawsuit was carried out maliciously and without basis in fact. The company demanded $250 dollars each from Looff and the bank financing him. The case was dismissed when the plaintiffs failed to appear in court. (Courtesy of PEMCO Webster and Stevens Collection, Museum of History and Industry, 1983.10.10289.)

Alki Beach Park, pictured here in 1912, occupied 2,500 feet of beach and quickly proved popular, sometimes attracting crowds of around 20,000. A bandstand was later built over the water, further increasing crowds. Over 100,000 people attended the concerts during the first season. (Courtesy of Special Collections, University of Washington Libraries, A. Curtis 35142.)

Alki Beach Park also included a bathing pavilion, which housed an indoor saltwater pool. The park became a new favorite destination for Sunday and holiday crowds, each season bringing a sizable increase in bathers. The new park's attendance rose, but Luna Park's declined. In the photograph below, a ferry bound for Alki Point passes by Luna Park. (Above, courtesy of PEMCO Webster and Stevens Collection, Museum of History and Industry, 1983.10.6779; below, courtesy of Special Collections, University of Washington Libraries, UW 29406z.)

Facing legal woes and foundering business, Charles I.D. Looff sold the Luna Park Amusement Company. In April 1913, the park's new manager announced a number of forthcoming renovations. The attractions were to be enlarged and the figure-eight coaster replaced with a racing coaster. Stock in the Luna Park Amusement Company was offered at $1,000 a share. The renovations never happened, and Luna Park closed later that year. One final lawsuit was filed against Luna Park in 1913. The City of Seattle sued the new manager for nonpayment of a $1,200 electric bill. (Courtesy of PEMCO Webster and Stevens Collection, Museum of History and Industry, 1983.10.10291.1.)

# Seven

# LAST OF LUNA PARK

Luna Park had only a brief career as an amusement park. By late 1914, a mostly vacant pier lingered where Seattle's Coney Island once stood. Almost two decades later, fire destroyed it. The headline in the *Seattle Times* read, "Fire Devours Last of Luna Park Building." The Luna Park pleasure pier was a loss, but traces of it remain to this day.

In 1914, Luna Park's carousel was installed at San Francisco's Playland at the Beach. The machine operated for almost 60 years, delighting new generations of pleasure seekers. Fortunately, the carousel has managed to remain completely intact; many such machines were broken up, their figures sold off individually. Looff's 1906 gem was fully restored and now runs in San Francisco's South of Market neighborhood.

The site where Luna Park stood is one of the most scenic in Seattle. From this vista, the faint blue profile of the Olympic Mountains can be seen, as well as the remarkable cityscape from Magnolia Bluff to downtown. For close to two decades, the site was vacant, an obtrusive concrete pit flanked by gnarled pilings. Not until the early 1950s was the pool filled in and the pilings removed. It was another 50 years before the site was renovated into the public park that stands there today.

Memories of Luna Park persist. Visitors of its original site are treated to a synopsis of the park's history etched in cement. The nearby Luna Park Café, which took its name from the park's restaurant, also serves as a landmark of sorts. Even the restaurant's surrounding neighborhood has been named Luna Park. The vestiges of the park itself are its few surviving pilings, which are most often hidden beneath the waves.

Luna Park's only remaining structures were the natatorium and dance hall. The pier lingered while the surrounding city modernized. The photograph above shows Elliott Bay from the shipping district in the early 1930s, with the Luna Park pier in the distance. The natatorium was renamed Luna Pool, and some of the slot machines, which had been such a problem before, were set up in the lobby. In 1927, a swim team, the Luna Swimming Club, was formed. In 1930, fifty Seattle children were awarded Red Cross badges for their proficiency in the water. They had received their instruction at Luna Pool. (Above, author's collection; below, courtesy of Southwest Seattle Historical Society/Log House Museum.)

In March 1924, with Prohibition in effect, Luna Park was again entangled with vice. Federal agents opened fire on two speedboats, such as the one pictured above, during a late-night liquor raid at the pier. One of the boats disappeared in the darkness. The Coast Guard cutter *Scout* apprehended the other. Piloting the captured speedboat was a former customs agent who had been convicted of smuggling narcotics and already had a liquor charge pending against him. Agents took axes to the doors of Luna Park's pavilion and searched a trailer parked outside. In all, they seized 75 cases of bonded liquor. (Above, courtesy of Museum of History and Industry, SHS 17111; below, courtesy of Puget Sound Maritime Historical Society, PSMHS 764.)

During the early hours of April 14, 1931, Luna Pool caught fire. Flames shot 100 feet in the air, and the pier blazed across the bay one final time. The natatorium and dance hall were completely destroyed, along with 800 brand-new bathing suits. The assistant fire marshal initially attributed the fire to a discarded match or cigarette smoldering and eventually breaking into flame, but it was eventually determined to have been the work of an arsonist. (Courtesy of Southwest Seattle Historical Society/Log House Museum.)

The remains of Luna Park's natatorium, seen in this 1940s photograph, continued making headlines for the next 20 years. Unpaid taxes placed the parcel of land, considered one of the most beautiful in Seattle, into the hands of the King County Property Department. The City of Seattle was among several parties wishing to acquire the site, which it finally did in 1945. (Courtesy of Seattle Municipal Archives.)

The decaying pilings around the site, seen in this 1940s aerial photograph, were a hazard to those who fished from them and an eyesore to most others. In the early 1950s, the city declared it would replace the rotting pilings with a public fishing pier. The pilings were removed and the cement pools filled in, but no pier was built. Not until 2004, when the city removed the concrete seawall to make way for a new park, did any major construction take place at the site. (Courtesy of Seattle Municipal Archives.)

With the closing of Luna Park, the *City of Seattle*, which had ferried thousands to the pleasure pier, was sold. In the photograph above, the name of the vessel's new owner is painted on the side. By 1919, the streetcar system was no longer profitable and was sold to the city. The city ran the lines until 1940 and then began dismantling the tracks. The last car, providing service to Ballard, made its final run in 1941. The streetcars were subsequently burned and their metal used for scrap. (Above, courtesy of Special Collections, University of Washington Libraries, UW 7706; below, courtesy of Seattle Post-Intelligencer Collection, Museum of History and Industry, PI 27166.)

On August 13th, 1951, the disreputable resort on Beacon Hill was destroyed when a B-50 Superfortress crashed into it. The resort's original rooms had been renovated into multiroom dwellings, and the building was named the Lester Apartments. Its proximity to Boeing made it a convenient residence for workers. The bomber had been passing over from the nearby airfield when it developed engine problems. (Both, courtesy of Seattle Post-Intelligencer Collection, Museum of History and Industry, PI 020240, PI 20247.)

Luna Park's carousel was installed at San Francisco's Playland at the Beach. The 10-acre amusement park, located on the western edge of the city, had begun as a squatters' settlement in the 19th century. The photograph above, taken in 1914, shows the exterior of the carousel's hippodrome, which had a similar design to the one at Luna Park. In 1949, Looff's carousel, shown below, was still popular with riders of all ages. The machine was a highlight of the park, which had been renamed Whitney's Playland in 1928. (Above, courtesy of James R. Smith; below, courtesy of San Francisco History Center, San Francisco Public Library.)

By the 1970s, the hippodrome had been remodeled and renamed the merry-go-round. This 1972 photograph shows the hippodrome next to the Fun House, another of Playland's attractions. It was built in the early 1920s and housed a Laffing Sal, a mechanical clown famous for its raucous laughter. (Courtesy of Dennis O'Rorke, San Francisco's Playland at the Beach.)

After decades of rousing young imaginations, Looff's carousel still retained its luster, and the detailing of the machine's figures was just as striking as it had been during its days at Luna Park. (Courtesy of David Johnson Collection of San Francisco Photography.)

This photograph was one of the last taken of the Looff carousel at Playland. The 1972 season was Playland's last, and it closed after Labor Day. Looff's machine had been a fixture at the amusement park for close to 60 years. (Courtesy of San Francisco History Center, San Francisco Public Library.)

The carousel was sold in its entirety at auction to a private collector, which prevented it from being sold in pieces. It was stored for a few years and then moved to Long Beach, California, where it operated for more than a decade. (Courtesy of San Francisco History Center, San Francisco Public Library.)

In 1998, the Looff carousel was purchased by San Francisco's Redevelopment Agency as part of an urban renewal project in the South of Market neighborhood. The machine was fully restored and installed in a modernized hippodrome on the rooftop of Yerba Buena Gardens, where it remains a popular attraction. (Photograph by Shoji Mita.)

Children's Creativity Museum in San Francisco now operates Looff's machine. Formerly Zeum: San Francisco's Children's Museum, it was constructed as part of the same urban renewal project and offers hands-on activities in multimedia arts and technology, as well as community exhibit space and a 200-seat theater. The nonprofit museum is visited by over 250,000 youth annually. (Photograph by Matt Granz Photography; courtesy of Children's Creativity Museum.)

The carousel is one of about twelve hand-carved Looff machines still in operation. Its figures embody a bygone era of American craftsmanship. The four-row menagerie continues to stir the imaginations and cheer the hearts of its riders. More than a century old, the carousel is delighting a new generation and continuing the joyful legacy of Charles I.D. Looff. (Above, photograph by David H.M. Spector; below, photograph by Francesca D'Alessio, courtesy of Children's Creativity Museum.)

The Luna Park Café opened on March 18, 1989. The venue was named in the park's honor and is decorated throughout with images of the former attraction. The restaurant's original building opened after World War II as Klaas Tavern. It was built on the site of a former gas station, which can be seen in the early photograph at right. The station was run by the Boysen family, as were the grocery store and the apartments next door. (Above, photograph by author; right, courtesy of John Bennett.)

Luna Park's site had become known as Anchor Park in the 1950s, named for the two-and-a-half-ton anchor that was dredged up just off the shore and put on display. By 2004, the park's original seawall was badly eroded. Rather than repair it, the city had it removed and built a pier in its place. The anchor was included, and the site remains a stunning vantage point. The etching and marker pictured below indicate where Looff's carousel once stood. (Both, photograph by author.)

When the tide along Alki Beach retreats far enough, the last remnants of Luna Park's pilings are revealed. Juxtaposed against present-day downtown, they tell the story of a much different Seattle. With the tide this low, it is common to spot beachcombers scouring the flats with metal detectors, hoping to unearth lost and forgotten relics. When the tide returns, the ruins are hidden beneath the bay once more, and "the Nation's Greatest Playground on the Pacific Coast" drifts back into memory. (Photograph by Russell Bernice.)

# SELECTED BIBLIOGRAPHY

Berner, Richard C. *Seattle 1900–1920: From Boomtown, Urban Turbulence, to Restoration*. Seattle: Charles Press, 1991.

Dinger, Charlotte. *Art of the Carousel*. Green Village, NJ: Carousel Art, Inc., 1983.

Dorpat, Paul. *Seattle, Now and Then*. Seattle: Tartu Publications, 1984.

Eals, Clay, ed. *West Side Story*. Seattle: Robinson Newspapers, 1987.

Eklund, Donald D. *Washington's "Wild Scotsman": The Early Aeronautical Adventures of L. Guy Mecklem, 1897–1910*. Bellingham, WA: Center for Pacific Northwest Studies, 1974.

Evans, Sondra, ed. "The Looff Dynasty." *Carousel Art*, no. 14 (August 1981): 3–9.

Filer, Patricia. *All Aboard for Luna Park*. Seattle: Southwest Seattle Historical Society, 2000.

Fraley, Tobin. *The Great American Carousel: A Century of Master Craftsmanship*. San Francisco: Chronicle Books, 1994.

Fried, Frederick. *A Pictorial History of the Carousel*. New York: A.S. Barnes and Company, 1964.

Hendrick, Burton J. "The 'Recall' in Seattle." *McClure's Magazine* (October 1911): 647–663.

Mangels, William F. *The Outdoor Amusement Industry: From Earliest Times to the Present*. New York: Vantage Press, Inc., 1952.

Manns, William, Peggy Shank, and Marianne Stevens. *Painted Ponies: American Carousel Art*. New York: Zon International Publishing Company, 1986.

*Seattle Post-Intelligencer*. "Many Drunken Girls and Boys at Luna Park." January 31, 1911.

Stein, Alan J., and Marie McCaffrey. "Seattle 1907: A Milestone Year," essay 8244 (August 2007). http://historylink.org.

Warren, James R. *Seattle: An Illustrated History*. Woodland Hills, CA: Windsor Publications, Inc., 1981.

# INDEX

Alki Beach Park, 99, 108, 109
Alki Point Natatorium, 45
Anchor Park, 124
Baldwin, Thomas Scott, 52, 78
*California Arrow*, 78
Canals of Venice, 13, 26, 33, 34, 43
carousel
    Children's Creativity Museum, 121, 122
    Coney Island, Brooklyn, 36, 65–67
    Luna Park, Seattle, 11, 17, 33–38, 68, 70,
       72, 111, 118, 124
    Natatorium Park, Spokane, 70
    Playland, San Francisco, 111, 118–120
    The Pike, Long Beach, 74
Christofferson, Harry, 32
Chutes Park, Los Angeles, California, 77–79
*City of Seattle* ferry, 20, 21, 116
Coney Island, Brooklyn, New York, 2, 7, 9,
    15, 18, 25, 36, 40, 65–67
Crescent Park, Riverside, Rhode Island, 35, 68
Diavlo, 55
Dilling, George W., 94, 97, 98
Elliott Bay, 2, 7, 8, 15, 17, 21, 40, 45, 83,
    90, 100, 112
Feltman, Charles, 67
Gill, Hiram C., 87, 92–94, 97, 98
Great Figure-Eight Roller Coaster, 2, 33, 38
Joy Wheel, 44
Kuhn Brothers, the, 60
Leschi Park, 75
Looff
    Arthur, 38, 73, 74
    carousel, 8, 11, 17, 33–38, 65–68, 70,

      72–74, 111, 118–122, 124
    Charles I.D., 11, 17, 27, 33, 35–38, 49, 54,
      56, 65–75, 99, 104–107, 110, 122
    William, 69, 70, 106
Luna Park
    Amusement Company, 99, 102, 110
    Café (modern), 8, 111, 123
    Café (original), 17, 96
    Cleveland, Ohio, 19
    Coney Island, New York, 15, 18
    Pittsburgh, Pennsylvania, 19
    Seattle, Washington, 2, 7–11, 13–18, 21–65,
      68–73, 75, 80, 82–88, 90, 91, 95, 96, 98–105,
      109–113, 115, 116, 119, 124, 125
    streetcar line, Seattle, 22–24
Luna Pool, 8, 112, 114
May, Angela, 60, 61
Mecklem, Llewellyn Guy, 63, 75–86
Meeker, Ezra, 33, 50, 51
Natatorium, Luna Park, Seattle, 8, 17, 26,
    45–47, 99, 105, 110, 112, 114, 115
Oscillating swing, 2, 26, 28, 33, 34, 42
Playland at the Beach (Playland), San Francisco,
    California, 111, 118–120
roller coaster, 38, 39, 80
Seattle
    Electric Company, 16, 22
    Park Company, 10, 17, 70, 88, 91, 99, 104–107
Shoot-the-Chutes, 2, 8, 9, 17, 33, 34, 40, 41,
    63, 103
"Uncle Hiram" (Carl Hinckley), 48, 49, 61
Wappenstein, Charles ("Wappy"), 92, 95, 98

# www.arcadiapublishing.com

Discover books about the town where you grew up, the cities where your friends and families live, the town where your parents met, or even that retirement spot you've been dreaming about. Our Web site provides history lovers with exclusive deals, advanced notification about new titles, e-mail alerts of author events, and much more.

Find Your Place in History.